Especially for

_____

From

_____

Date

_____

Christmas Prayers

A Keepsake Devotional for the Holiday Season

RENAE BRUMBAUGH

BARBOUR

PUBLISHING

Published by Barbour Publishing, Inc., P.O. Box 719, Uhrichsville, Ohio 44683
www.barbourbooks.com

Our mission is to publish and distribute inspirational products offering exceptional value and biblical encouragement to the masses.

 Member of the
Evangelical Christian
Publishers Association

Printed in China.

Contents

Introduction 7

Prayers for Peace **9**
Reassurance 10
Mission Impossible? 13
Because of Jesus 14
Walls 17
Finding Peace 18
Pursuit 21
Finding Strength 22
Sweet Dreams 25
Birth Announcement 26
Pine Trees 29

Prayers for Wisdom **31**
Surprise, Surprise! 32
Warned 35
Descendent 36
Because of Him 39
Mystery 40
The Beginning of Wisdom 43
Lasting Joy 44
When Opportunity Knocks 47
Unbelievable 48
Signs 51

Prayers for Relationships 53
Love in Action 54
Everyone Wins. 57
Change in Plans 58
Giving Generously 61
Finding Joy 62
Old Woman 65
Another Route 66
Spread the Word 69
Gentle and Kind 70
This Is Love 73

Prayers of Gratitude 75
Thank You 76
Great Expectations. 79
What's in a Name? 80
Getting Noticed 83
Good Gifts 84
God with Us 87
Extravagant Gift 88
Overjoyed 91
Promises Kept 92
Three Little Words 95

End of Season Prayer 96

INTRODUCTION

When I was a little girl, and even after I was a big girl, Christmas held a special wonder for me. Like many little girls and boys, I was fascinated by the lights, the music, and the beautifully wrapped gifts. I looked forward to the Christmas specials that played on one of our three television stations. I took part in various Christmas productions, both at church and at school. One year I played the Christmas tree.

Yep. Green stockings and all.

Many of my fondest memories are ones that, try as I may, I'll never be able to duplicate. The color wheel that made our tree turn from red to green to blue to white. . .and that made a constant humming noise. The scraping of occasional light snow with a rake off our Texas lawn to make a pitiful version of Frosty the Snowman. The yearly trip to the Christmas tree lot with my daddy to pick out a tree. . .tall or short? Fat or skinny? Flocked or plain? These pages from my mental scrapbook are tucked safely away, cherished, never to be forgotten.

Though my fascination with this season's trappings has faded a bit, there's one thing that still holds my awe and brings me to my knees: that Name. You know the One I speak of. The Name that is above every name. The Name that will cause every knee to bow and every tongue to confess that He is Lord.

It is my prayer that the words in this book will help you experience the true wonder of the season—the miracle of God's gift to us: *Jesus.*

A Christmas Prayer

Dear Father,

Festive lights, joyful music, and beautifully adorned trees are everywhere. These are symbols of the season, intended as reminders of Your peace, Your joy, and Your love. Yet no human effort can accurately convey the kind of love it took to send Your Son as a payment, a sacrifice for mankind. Your love is beyond understanding, Your gift too extravagant for us to ever repay. All we can offer in return is our hearts. Humble as our gift to You may be, we offer it still, arms outstretched, heads bowed.

Merry Christmas, Father. Amen.

Prayers
for Peace

Reassurance

*But the angel said to her, "Do not be afraid, Mary, you have found favor
with God. You will be with child and give birth to a son,
and you are to give him the name Jesus."*
LUKE 1:30–31

Poor Mary. There she was, sound asleep in her bed, when all of
a sudden she heard a loud voice—a man's voice—coming from
somewhere in the room. She startled awake only to find a bright light.
Squinting against it, she made out the silhouette of a man—but not a
man. Something different. Talk about a nightmare.

But wait! What was the creature saying? "Do not be afraid. You
have found favor with God."

We all feel afraid sometimes. At times our circumstances seem
overwhelming, even terrifying. But with God, we never have to
feel afraid. He created us, He thinks we are special, and He has a
wonderful plan for each of our lives. Often we want to fight against
our circumstances. We want to run and hide, or tell God to find
somebody else. But God is all-knowing, all-wise, and all-loving. He
will never lead us into more than we can handle. And He will always,
always walk with us every step of the way.

Many times it is through our most frightening events that God
brings the greatest blessings. Instead of feeling afraid, we can learn
from Mary. We can say, "Yes, Lord. I will do whatever You say."

Dear Father,

Thank You for sending Your Son to be the Prince of Peace. I can only imagine how Mary must have felt when she heard that You had chosen her to be His mother. Frightened, excited, shocked—anything but peaceful. Sometimes I feel those things, too. I want to run and hide from my circumstances; I want to say, "No, Lord. Find somebody else to go through this." But I know You love me and have a beautiful plan for my life.

Father, help me to trust You when I feel anxious and afraid. Help me to say yes to Your plan for my life, and to draw on the peace that comes from Your Son. Amen.

Dear Father,

It seems impossible for a young virgin to bear a child—especially when that child is Your own Son. Yet You worked a miracle, and Jesus was born. It seems impossible that You would sacrifice that child for the likes of me. Yet You did. Thank You, Lord.

Father, there are things in my life that seem hopeless and impossible. When I think about them, I feel anxious and discouraged. Help me to remember that You can do anything. Nothing is impossible with You. Even when faced with life's most challenging trials, I can relax, knowing that there is no challenge too difficult for You. Amen.

Mission Impossible

"Even Elizabeth your relative is going to have a child in her old age, and she who was said to be barren is in her sixth month. For nothing is impossible with God." "I am the Lord's servant," Mary answered. "May it be to me as you have said." Then the angel left her.
LUKE 1:36–38

Sometimes things just don't make sense. When we are faced with impossible, unfair situations, we may feel confused and discouraged. Things like cancer, divorce, job loss, death, and other things can leave us feeling defeated and hopeless.

But with God, we never need to feel hopeless. God can move mountains. He can heal the sick and give sight to the blind. He can cause an elderly, barren woman to become pregnant. He can even cause a virgin to bear His own child. Nothing is impossible with Him.

When the impossible looms over us, we can choose to respond just as Mary did. We can say, "Lord, I don't understand this. It doesn't make any sense to me. But I trust You anyway." We can have peace in the midst of chaos, knowing that God knows what He's doing. He has good plans for our lives, and He has everything under control.

Because of Jesus

We have peace with God through our Lord Jesus Christ.
ROMANS 5:1

The loudspeaker blared the words "Sleep in heavenly peace..." But the words to the famous Christmas carol seemed almost ironic. After all, crowds were pushing against one another. Babies were crying, and to my left two women argued over who had the rights to the last Luau Barbie.

Directly in front of me were Hot Wheels in every conceivable color. Which one would my nephew want more—red or blue? My head pounded with the triviality of it all. Though Christmas is hailed as the holiday of peace, sometimes it seems anything but peaceful. Good thing God didn't send Jesus to give us a peaceful shopping experience, or even a peaceful, snow-covered holiday. No, the peace that Jesus brings has nothing to do with the weather or the music or the gifts.

Jesus came to give us lasting peace. He left His throne in heaven so we could have peace with God. Though our circumstances may change, though the loudspeakers may blare and our headaches may pound...we can know peace in the midst of it. We can have peace, not because of our surroundings, but because He has placed His peace within us. Because of Jesus, we can have God's peace in our hearts.

Dear Father,

This world can be noisy, crowded, and cold. Circumstances press in and try to steal any hope I have of finding hope and rest and tranquility. Sometimes peace seems out of reach.

Yet I know I can find peace anytime, anyplace. I don't have to look very far, either! Because of Jesus, I can have Your peace within my heart. Because of Jesus, I can hold Your hand and lay my head on Your shoulder. I can talk to You, and You will listen. I can be carried along by Your love.

Because of Jesus, I can have a good relationship with You, the Almighty God. Because of Jesus, I know peace. Amen.

Dear Father,

It's easy to pray for world peace. After all, world peace doesn't require much of me. It takes place somewhere on the other side of the globe and only affects me as I watch the evening news.

But I know You brought peace to my life so that I can carry it to those around me. Please help me to tear down the walls of anger and hostility that may be erected around my life—in my community, my church, my neighborhood, and even in my home. Help me to remember the words to the familiar Christmas song: "Let there be peace on earth, and let it begin in me." Amen.

Walls

For he himself is our peace,
who has...destroyed the...dividing wall of hostility.
EPHESIANS 2:14

For a short time I lived in a rural southern town where the racial divisions were rarely mentioned but where you could cut the tension with a knife. Though no one ever said the words out loud, the unwritten code was clear: The races didn't mix. They had their churches, their hangouts, their neighborhoods; and we had ours.

The early church faced the same difficulties. There were Jews and there were Greeks, and the two groups weren't supposed to mix. Then Christ came, and He turned the cultural stereotypes upside down! He tore down the walls, broke through the barriers, and brought peace.

Because of Christ, we can have peace with people of other races. We can have peace with people who don't think like we do. We can live at peace even with those who don't believe in Christ, for it is only through Christ that we can experience the gentleness, humility, and love that will bring true peace to the world.

At Christmastime and all year long, we need to look for ways to tear down the walls of hostility and hatred in our homes, our communities, and our world. He is our peace...and He wants to bring peace to those around us, as well.

Finding Peace

"Peace I leave with you; my peace I give you. I do not give to you as the world gives. Do not let your hearts be troubled and do not be afraid."
JOHN 14:27

If you ask people at the shopping mall or on the street today to define peace, many of them will tell you it is the absence of conflict. To have peace, we often feel we must remove ourselves from the source of our stress. When we arrive at a place without stress and conflict, we think we'll find peace.

The problem is, no such place exists—at least not here on earth. Oh, we may find temporary peace by changing jobs or changing relationships or planning a beach retreat. But it won't last. It never does.

Jesus offers a different kind of peace. His peace is in spite of circumstances, not because of them. The peace of God travels with us, inhabiting our hearts and minds no matter what is going on around us. When we draw on His peace, we can find tranquility even in the midst of conflict. His peace is there for the taking; all we have to do is claim it, as we call on Him.

Dear Father,

I'm so glad You don't give as the world gives. As I purchase gifts for my family and friends this holiday season, I know that my gifts are an imperfect reminder of my love for them. Each gift will grow old or run out, and next year I'll purchase new gifts. But Your gifts are eternal, and they begin the moment we accept them.

Thank You for the gift of Your peace, which I can access any time, simply by calling on You. I'm glad that Your peace can be found even in the most stressful of situations, even in the midst of chaos and conflict. Thank You, Father, for Your peace. Please help me to be a messenger of that peace, carrying it to those I love. Amen.

Dear Father,

Thank You for making Your peace available to me. I know it is within my reach; all I have to do is accept it. But pursuing peace. . . responding with peace in the midst of conflict. . .that's another story.

Help me to be a peacemaker. Help me to pursue peace by responding in love, gentleness, and humility to the stressful situations around me. I know that You want to use me as a messenger of Your peace in this world.

Remind me to be a beacon of Your love and gentleness to everyone—including those people who cause me stress. I know that by carrying Your peace to others, I obtain it for myself, as well. Amen.

Pursuit

Turn from evil and do good; seek peace and pursue it.
PSALM 34:14

Have you ever met a person who didn't want peace? Probably not. The desire for a peaceful existence is innate; for the most part, we all want to live tranquil, stress-free lives. That's one reason everyone loves Christmas. The season brings promises of peace.

The problem is that we want peace to come to us. We want the people around us to be nice to us. We want our jobs to fall into place, without us having to do much.

Unfortunately, life doesn't work that way. If we want peace, we have to pursue it. If we want peace, we have to find it within ourselves. Easier said than done.

It isn't easy to respond in a gentle tone when someone is yelling at us. But we must, if we want peace. It isn't easy to take up the slack for a coworker who isn't doing his or her share, but we must. In so doing, we pursue peace.

God's peace is available to all who seek it. We must carry it with us—not just at Christmas, but all year long. If we are to have peace, we must practice peace. When we pursue God's peace, we find it for ourselves, and we also deliver it to those around us who need it so desperately.

Finding Strength

The LORD gives strength to his people;
the LORD blesses his people with peace.
PSALM 29:11

The phone bill was due yesterday. The car needs new tires, and the toilet keeps overflowing. On top of it all, the kids need new shoes, and the Christmas gifts aren't bought yet. And now in the rearview mirror are those telltale flashing lights. The last thing we need is a speeding ticket. Maybe the officer will show some holiday spirit and just give a warning.

On days like that, it's easy to lose our temper and blow our cool. We bark at our kids and growl at our spouse, and they learn quickly to just stay out of our way. Maintaining a calm, gentle spirit takes more strength than we feel we have.

But God gives us the strength we need to respond to every situation the way He would respond. The same strength that parted the Red Sea, the same strength that caused the King of the universe to be born in a manger, is the strength that is available to each one of His children. We may feel overwhelmed, but God offers His peace in the midst of life's chaos. He holds it out to us; all we have to do is accept it. No matter what our circumstances, we can remain calm, because His strength dwells within us.

Dear Father,

Sometimes Your peace seems absent from me. When the walls of my life cave in, I want to run and hide. Instead of drawing on Your strength, I feel frustrated and afraid, and I don't always respond as I should.

I'm so glad to know that the same strength that calmed the sea, healed the sick, and brought Christ back from death is available to me. That strength allows me to overcome any situation, instead of allowing the situation to control me. Because of that strength, I can respond to my circumstances with gentleness, peace, and love. When life gets hard, help me to remember Your peace. Amen.

Dear Father,

Sometimes sleep evades me. Worry and stress keep my muscles tense and my mind active, and I lie in bed, wide awake, for hours. Yet I know that's not what You want for me. That's why You sent Jesus—so I could know peace.

Father, You've already done everything that is needed for me to feel safe, loved, and protected. Though the circumstances around me may feel out of control, I know You are right there. You stand ready to protect me, comfort me, and surround me with Your love. Thank You for Your peace in the midst of chaos.

Thank You that I can sleep peacefully, knowing You have everything under control. Amen.

Sweet Dreams

I pulled the covers over my head and hummed a Christmas carol, trying to block out the sounds of gunfire going off right across the freeway. Living near a military installation makes me feel safe. After all, if the bad guys come calling, I have a gazillion soldiers right outside my front door, waiting to protect me. But the sounds of war aren't peaceful, no matter how you look at it.

Years of hearing those sounds have taught me to tune out the military practice that takes place so close to home. Our soldiers know what they're doing, and I know they won't cast any bombs in my direction. Now I can even sleep through those sounds.

War isn't peaceful; yet the sounds of soldiers preparing for war is reassuring. They stand ready to protect us, practicing their strategies at all hours of the night so the rest of us can sleep peacefully. We don't have to worry about the boogeyman.

God stands ready, twenty-four hours a day, to protect us. He is mighty and powerful, and He's prepared to defend His children. I can sleep peacefully, knowing my Father is watching over me. After all, He is stronger than the enemy, and He loves me with all His heart. He will take care of me.

I don't have to worry about a thing.

Birth Announcement

Wow! Talk about an impressive birth announcement. Angels filled the sky, singing glorious praises about the newborn Son of God. Their song has been the inspiration for countless hymns, carols, and symphonies ever since. Though their music was undoubtedly the most beautiful chorus ever heard, it wasn't the melody or the chords or the harmony that gave this song its eternal appeal.

It was the message.

Since the fall of man in the Garden of Eden, we have been striving to find peace. We convince ourselves that if we could just have a better job or a fancier house or nicer friends, we'd have peace. We reach for those goals, but they never seem to bring us the fulfillment they promised. Peace, the real, lasting kind, can't be manufactured by human circumstances. True peace comes only from having a right relationship with God.

On that glorious, starry night, God showed favor to mankind. He made a way for us to finally stop reaching, to finally grab hold of the hand of God. He sent His Son, who provided a way for us to reconcile with God.

On that beautiful, music-filled night, God sent Peace.

Dear Father,

Thank You for the gift of music. This season, as I hear carols playing in the background, I'm reminded of Your love, Your joy, and Your peace. I'm so thankful that You loved me enough to provide a way for me to find real, lasting peace.

All around me are people who have never discovered Your peace. As I learn to take advantage of the peace You've made available to me, help me to share it with others. As they watch the way I respond to circumstances with the calm assurance that can only come from You, may they long for Your peace in their own lives.

Thank You for Your peace, Lord. Amen.

Dear Father,

Thank You for Your gifts of joy and peace. I know that You want my life to be peaceful, like a whispering pine. You want it to be joyful, like the music I hear at Christmas. Yet much of my life isn't peaceful. It often seems I encounter briars and thorns at every turn.

Help me to stay close to You, Father. Help me to talk to You in constant prayer. Help me to listen to what You say in Your Word. I long to experience that pathway of whispering pines that You have prepared for me.

I love You. Amen.

Pine Trees

Pine Trees

"You will go out in joy and be led forth in peace....
Instead of the thornbush will grow the pine tree."
ISAIAH 55:12–13

There's a reason we decorate pine trees at Christmastime. We fragrance our homes with the scent of pine; we use pine boughs to form wreaths; we sprinkle pine needles in our fireplaces to provide a comforting pop and sizzle. We place our gifts beneath our decorated pine tree, and we sing carols around it.

The pine tree has long been a symbol of peace. Poets have written about the whispering pines and their calming, soothing effect on the soul. While much of life seems to bring briars and thorns, God wants us to walk in a path of whispering pines—a path of peace. All we have to do is walk with Him, following Him daily as we spend time with Him through prayer and His Word.

God wants us to take the spirit of Christmas with us every day of the year, for the rest of our lives, and the Bible tells us we can. His promises of joy and peace aren't lofty, distant ideals, like carrots dangling just beyond our reach. They are gifts He holds out to us, eagerly waiting for us to reach out and take them.

Prayers for Wisdom

Surprise, Surprise!

But after he had considered this, an angel of the Lord appeared to him in a dream and said, "Joseph son of David, do not be afraid to take Mary home as your wife, because what is conceived in her is from the Holy Spirit. She will give birth to a son, and you are to give him the name Jesus, because he will save his people from their sins."
MATTHEW 1:20–21

Sometimes life just doesn't make sense. If we do what we are supposed to do, honor God, obey the laws, and pay our taxes, things are supposed to go well for us. Right?

It would be nice if life always went the way we expect it to. Unfortunately, that's not the way life works. Occasionally God throws us a curve ball, and we have to be ready. We must be willing to accept the surprises He sends, or we will miss the blessings that come along with those surprises.

Joseph obeyed God, even when life didn't make sense. Because of his willingness to roll with the punches, he received one of the greatest blessings anyone has ever received. He got to be Jesus' dad. God has great things in store for each of us, as well. We simply have to be willing to receive those surprises when life doesn't work out as we expected.

Dear Father,

Sometimes You surprise me. When things don't go as I expected, I often feel disappointed. If I had my way, my life would be ordered and perfect and. . .dull. But I know that You have bigger plans for me than I have for myself. You have chosen the path for me that will bring me closest to You. Often it's those unexpected paths in life that lead us to the greatest blessings.

Please help me to be like Joseph and accept the blessings You send, even when they don't come in the expected packages. I want to follow You, even when life doesn't make sense. I know I can trust You to lead me to the place of greatest blessing—the place that is nearest to You. Amen.

Dear Father,

Thank You for Your whispers of wisdom. I know that as long as I am seeking You, staying in Your Word, and drawing near to You, You will guide me in the way I should go. Help me to keep my spirit tuned to You, so I don't miss the gentle things You are saying to me.

Help me to act on Your quiet leadings, and not dismiss them as my imagination. I know that You will never lead me to do something that is contrary to Your written Word. Give me the kind of faith that Joseph had, obeying You even when it isn't convenient. I know I can trust that You will always lead me in the way that's best for me, and best for those I love. Amen.

Warned

Now when they had gone, behold, an angel of the Lord appeared to Joseph in a dream and said, "Get up! Take the Child and His mother and flee to Egypt, and remain there until I tell you; for Herod is going to search for the Child to destroy Him."
MATTHEW 2:13 NASB

What if Joseph had ignored this warning? What if he'd awakened and said, "Wow. What a nightmare. I'm glad that was only a dream." Joseph knew in his spirit that the warning was more than a dream. Deep in his soul, he knew God was trying to take care of him and his family. Joseph heeded the warning and fled to Egypt, and his wife and child were safe.

We've all had them—those little nudgings, those feelings that we should do something, call someone, or act in a certain way. All too often we ignore those feelings as irrational. While we shouldn't act on every impulse, we need to be sensitive to the Holy Spirit's leading. After all, He doesn't often give us flashing neon signs telling us what to do. More often He speaks to us through His Word, and through the gentle whispers we hear in our souls.

God's directions to us aren't always easy or convenient. Joseph had to leave the rest of his family and his business behind, in order to follow God's leading. Yet Joseph was a man of faith, and he knew God would never steer him in the wrong direction.

Descendent

A shoot will come up from the stump of Jesse;
from his roots a Branch will bear fruit.
The Spirit of the LORD will rest on him—
the Spirit of wisdom and of understanding
ISAIAH 11:1–2

Centuries before Jesus was born, God promised His people that He'd send a Savior, and that Savior would come from King David's lineage. Sure enough, Jesus came, just as God promised. That's why Matthew took such special care, in chapter 1, to recite Jesus' family tree through Joseph. Luke traced Mary's lineage in chapter 3. Both Mary and Joseph were descendents of David, so there was no question that Jesus was the promised Messiah.

One of the great things about Jesus was His wisdom. Even as a twelve-year-old boy in the temple, He astounded the wisest and most educated men of that culture. Then, when Jesus died, He promised to leave His Spirit with us—the same Spirit of wisdom and understanding that is referred to in this verse. When life seems confusing, we can call on God, and the same Spirit of wisdom that directed Jesus will direct us. His wisdom is a gift that keeps on giving—at Christmastime and all year long.

Dear Father,

Thank You for sending the same Spirit of wisdom and understanding to me that rested on Jesus. Forgive me for the times I forget to seek Your wisdom, for I know it's available to me anytime I ask. Thank You for making Your wisdom so clear to me in Your Word.

Father, this Christmas, as I give gifts to those I care about, I want to ask for a special gift from You—Your wisdom. Give me special insight into Your Word, and make me wise in all my ways. Help me to think, act, and speak with Your wisdom, as I seek to honor You in my life. Amen.

Dear Father,

Thank You for giving me wisdom. Thank You for reminding me that I don't have to know it all. As long as I'm looking to You, I'll always be headed in the right direction, because You will lead me in the way I should go.

It is such a relief to know that even when I feel confused and perplexed, I can relax. You will be wisdom for me, if I will only allow You to be in control. Father, today I want to step back and allow You to take the driver's seat of my life. Help me to surrender to Your wisdom and guidance, instead of following my own thoughts and desires. Amen.

Because of Him

"It is because of him that you are in Christ Jesus, who has become for us wisdom from God—that is, our righteousness, holiness and redemption."
1 Corinthians 1:30

It seems that every day, no matter how well-prepared we think we are, something always comes up to challenge our wisdom. We can work and pray and study, and yet, boom! There it is. A situation that we have no idea how to handle.

Perhaps it's a demanding relationship. Perhaps it's an unexpected financial burden. Whatever it is, we find ourselves perplexed, scratching our heads in confusion. Sometimes we even stomp our feet and clench our fists in frustration.

It's a good thing we don't need to have all the answers. This verse tells us that when we aren't wise, Christ will be wise for us! When we have no idea how to proceed, Christ will show us.

Not only that, but He will allow us to respond in righteousness and holiness. We don't have to get angry or frustrated or anxious. We can simply stand back, stand still, and wait for Him to lead us. That's what He's there for—to be our road map when we don't know where to turn. He will show us the way.

Mystery

So that they may have the full riches of complete understanding,
in order that they may know the mystery of God, namely, Christ,
in whom are hidden all the treasures of wisdom and knowledge.
COLOSSIANS 2:2–3

Some of the greatest things about Christmastime are the mystery, the secrets, the sneaking around trying to pull one over on our loved ones so they won't guess what are in those boxes under the tree. We've even been known to wrap tiny gifts in huge boxes, or place a picture of a huge gift in a tiny box, just to throw them off. Mysteries are appealing, no matter who we are. But when we aren't able to solve the mystery, we become frustrated.

God doesn't want us to be frustrated. He wants us to know and understand Him. But God is so amazing, so incredible, so huge, He is beyond our human ability to comprehend. That's why He sent us a tutor—the Holy Spirit.

When we feel lost and confused, when we feel like the things of God are out of our reach, we can relax. All we have to do is call on Him, and He will send the Tutor. If we study His Word, if we push everything else aside and listen to Him with all of our hearts, we will find wisdom.

Mystery solved.

Dear Father,
Thank You for making it possible for me to understand Your wisdom.
Often I want to receive that wisdom and understanding without
studying or listening. I just want it to be there, without having to
work for it.

Yet just as a detective has to spend time searching out clues and
examining evidence in order to solve a mystery, I know I need to
spend time in prayer and in Your Word, learning all I can about Your
way of thinking. Help me to study diligently. Help me to be teachable.
I want to understand You, think like You, be like You. Thank You for
helping me solve the mystery of You. Amen.

Dear Jesus,

Forgive me for focusing too much on Your sweet innocence and not enough on Your power. The story of Your birth is such a beautiful one. Yet Your birth was only one small piece of Your amazing story. As a matter of fact, the end of the story is still being written.

I know that You are no longer a baby, sleeping peacefully in the hay. You are the Mighty God, and Satan flees at the sound of Your voice. I adore You, Jesus. I am in awe of You. I respect You and fear You. I love You with all of my heart. Amen.

The Beginning of Wisdom

The fear of the LORD is the beginning of wisdom; all who follow his precepts have good understanding. To him belongs eternal praise.
PSALM 111:10

Christmas brings images of a sweet baby boy, being lulled to sleep by his young mother. Stars shining brightly, angels singing in the background, cattle gently mooing. . . peaceful. Serene. Innocent.

Harmless.

It's a beautiful picture, but it's not a complete picture. That same baby who was rocked to sleep by His mother grew up. He lived a perfect, sinless life. He went toe to toe with some of the most powerful leaders of His culture, then endured excruciating torture to the point of death. Next, in an act of power unknown by any earthly creature, He flexed His awesome might and conquered sin, death, and evil. He is still alive and well today, and the demons tremble at the mention of His name. That baby—Jesus—deserves more than our sweet sentimentality and admiration. He is to be revered.

Most people admire Jesus. They think He was a good man. But do we fear Him? Do we recognize His awesome power? If we want to understand the important things in our lives, if we want to be truly wise, we must begin here. Fear Him. Revere Him. That is our first step to wisdom.

Lasting Joy

"These things I have spoken to you so that My joy may be in you, and that your joy may be made full."
JOHN 15:11 NASB

Most of us probably know the words to the famous Christmas carol "Joy to the World." We've heard it so many times, it almost becomes background noise for the holidays. Yet when Jesus came to earth, He really did make it possible for us to experience true joy.

Many of us feel that if we could just change our circumstances, we'd be happy. We long for better jobs, nicer houses, and fancier cars. Those things might make us smile for a little while. But that kind of happiness never lasts. The better job is more stressful than our old job. The nicer house also has a heftier mortgage payment. And the fancy car wears out just like its less expensive counterpart.

Jesus came so that we could have lasting joy. You see, happiness depends on our current circumstances and is only temporary. Joy, on the other hand, depends on our future. And as God's children, we can know for certain that our future is a bright one, filled with more joy than we can contain, for all of eternity.

Dear Father,
Thank You for sending Jesus so that I could know true and lasting joy.
I often forget that the things I long for, the things I think will bring
me happiness are often temporary pleasures. You want me to have a
deeper, more fulfilling joy than anything this world can offer.

This season, as I shop for gifts that will bring temporary happiness
to those I love, I pray they will also know the lasting joy that only You
can give. Help me to spread Your love and joy to all I meet. Give me
wisdom to look to You alone for fulfillment. Amen.

Dear Father,

Thank You for the example of the wise men. They saw an opportunity, and they acted on it. They didn't hesitate or make excuses. Because of their faith, You blessed them; they saw Jesus with their own eyes.

I wonder how many blessings I've missed, simply because I didn't take advantage of the opportunities You've sent my way. Next time You present me with a chance to do good, to spread Your Word or to share Your love, please help me to take it. I want to be wise. I want to act on Your will without hesitating, making the most of every opportunity. Amen.

When Opportunity Knocks

When Opportunity Knocks

Be very careful, then, how you live—not as unwise but as wise,
making the most of every opportunity.
Ephesians 5:15–16

I wonder what the wise men thought when they first saw the star that would lead them to God's Son. Sure, they'd studied the stars for years. They'd waited their whole lives for the fulfillment of God's promise to His people. But honestly! Studying is one thing. Packing your bags for a two-year journey—a journey that has no guarantee of leading you to your desired destination—is another thing entirely.

These men knew what it meant to make the most of every opportunity. They saw a chance—not a guarantee, but a *chance*—to see God's Son with their own eyes. And they took it. They didn't procrastinate or make excuses or come up with a list of pros and cons. Packing their bags, they left right away.

Many of us hear God's voice leading us one way or another, but we procrastinate. We hem-haw around (as my grandmother used to say), and we look for excuses not to act. When we do that, we miss the opportunities, as well as the blessings, that God has in store for us.

Unbelievable

But the angel said to them, "Do not be afraid. I bring you good news of great joy that will be for all the people. Today in the town of David a Savior has been born to you; he is Christ the Lord."
LUKE 2:10–11

The shepherds looked to the sky, their mouths hanging open. They had never been so terrified in all their lives! They had been coming to these fields every night for years, and nothing like this had ever happened. Bright lights, winged people in the sky, voices in the air. . .it was unbelievable.

Yet the angel reassured them. "Don't be afraid!"

Sometimes the things of God can feel pretty scary. His plans for our lives often lead us on unfamiliar journeys, and we can experience things that seem unbelievable. Some days we want to bury our faces under our pillows and squeeze our eyes shut. Other days we can't do much but stand and watch, our mouths hanging open.

God's message to us is the same: "Don't be afraid." God is love, and His plans for us are always good ones. Though we may feel terrified at what we see on the horizon, we can know that God is right there, He loves us, and He has something wonderful in store for our lives.

Dear Father,

Sometimes I feel afraid of what life brings my way. New and unfamiliar circumstances cause my jaw to drop and my heart to skip beats. Honestly, life terrifies me at times.

Yet I know You stand there, reaching out Your hand to me, whispering, "Don't be afraid, child." Just as those angels in the sky brought news that You were closer to those shepherds than ever before, I know my difficult circumstances can bring me closer to You than ever. All I have to do is calm down, take Your hand, and let You lead me through it. Help me to simply trust You. Amen.

Dear Father,

*Thank You for making Yourself known to me. Sometimes faith
is hard. Sometimes Your ways are difficult to believe, difficult to
understand. I suppose that's where faith comes in, isn't it? I can choose
to trust You, even when Your ways don't seem to make sense.*

*Help me to walk in faith. Help me to use Your Word as a road
map, as I search for Your perfect plans for my life. I know that I can
trust Your Word, even when I don't understand it. Thank You for
Your Holy Spirit, who helps me to understand You better. Amen.*

Signs

"This will be a sign to you: You will find a baby wrapped in cloths and lying in a manger."
LUKE 2:12

The shepherds didn't know what to think. Bright lights in the sky? Angels? God's Son, born nearby? It was too incredible to be true.

The angel knew they needed a sign. "Go see for yourselves!" the creature said. "You'll find Him wrapped in cloths and lying in a manger."

The shepherds had a choice. They could ignore the angel, keep their mouths shut, and pretend it was all just a strange dream. Or they could investigate for themselves, using the angel's words as a guide.

Sometimes we have a hard time knowing what to believe. But God always points the way, telling us what to look for. He sent His Word to show us the truth, and He sent His Holy Spirit to guide us. Sure, we'll have our doubts now and then, just like those shepherds. But if we are faithful to look to Him, God will always make Himself clear to us.

Like the shepherds, we each have a choice. We can ignore the signs He has given us, choosing to live in our own wisdom. Or we can choose a life of faith, as we search for God's purpose and plan, using His Word as a guide.

Prayers for
Relationships

Love in Action

If anyone has material possessions and sees his brother in need but has no pity on him, how can the love of God be in him? Dear children, let us not love with words or tongue but with actions and in truth.
1 John 3:17–18

During the holidays, it's easy to find ways to be charitable. On every corner there is a man in a Santa suit ringing a bell, asking for spare change to share with the needy. Local food banks have their annual food drives, and programs such as Coats for Kids advertise on the radio and television. We drop our change in the bucket, write our checks to our pet charities, and go on our merry ways. Giving to the needy makes us feel good about ourselves and adds to the holiday spirit.

It's funny, though. The needy are always with us. They don't just show up at Christmastime and suddenly become wealthy the rest of the year. So why do we often forget to be charitable in the spring and summer?

God wants us to look for ways to show our love no matter the season. He sees our needs even when they aren't obvious to the rest of the world, and finds creative ways to meet those needs. He wants us to imitate Him, always looking for people who need a touch of His love. He'll show us creative, compassionate ways to meet the needs of those around us, every day of the year.

Dear Father,
Please open my eyes to the needs of those around me. I often get caught up in my own troubles, and I forget to notice that people everywhere have bigger problems than I do. You have equipped me to help them, yet I often let their needs go unmet.

Lord, it is sometimes awkward knowing how to meet a need without making the person feel ashamed or embarrassed. Give me wisdom, and teach me to find creative ways to help the people You've placed in my path. I want to be an instrument of Your love and provision to all I meet, today and every day. Amen.

Dear Father,

Forgive me for my selfishness. I want to be noticed. I want to be important. I want everyone to think well of me. Lord, I'm so busy focusing on myself, I forget to notice the people around me.

Father, I know that true humility begins with recognition of who I am, both with You and without You. Without You, I am the lowest of sinners. Without You, I have no hope. But with You, Lord, I am somebody. I am a child of the King, with an enormous, immeasurable inheritance. Thank You for thinking of Me above Yourself. Help me to follow Your example, considering others' needs before my own. Amen.

Everyone Wins

Do nothing out of selfish ambition or vain conceit, but in humility consider others better than yourselves. Each of you should look not only to your own interests, but also to the interests of others.
Philippians 2:3–4

During the holiday season, selfishness is discouraged. After all, it's the season of giving. We are supposed to be generous and charitable. Yet the qualities that are encouraged during the holidays are often trampled the rest of the year.

If we want to be successful, we must step on—even squash—the competition. We need to look out for number one. To climb the ladder of success, we have to trample a few fingers, toes, and even hearts along the way. And that's okay, right? It's just the way things work.

But that's not part of God's design. Time and again in His Word, God tells us that if we want to be great, we must become small. That doesn't mean we have to be doormats, though. Truly it takes a strong person to put others' needs in front of his own. God knows that selfish ambition can destroy friendships, churches, companies, and even lives. Humility, on the other hand, brings people together and encourages unity. When true humility is present, everyone wins.

Change in Plans

This is how the birth of Jesus Christ came about: His mother Mary was pledged to be married to Joseph, but before they came together, she was found to be with child through the Holy Spirit. Because Joseph her husband was a righteous man and did not want to expose her to public disgrace, he had in mind to divorce her quietly.
MATTHEW 1:18–19

Mary and Joseph were in the midst of their wedding plans. They were probably spreading the word, making preparations for a huge feast, and sewing lovely wedding garments. Like most couples, they looked forward to beginning their lives together and starting a family.

Then they found out they'd be parents sooner than they expected. Joseph was devastated to learn the girl he loved was expecting a child that wasn't his. Yet he was a kind man and didn't want to humiliate her. He wanted to do the right thing, even though he felt he'd been wronged.

We can learn from Joseph. Sometimes, when we feel we've been mistreated, we respond in anger and hurt. We feel justified in our actions; because after all, we were the ones who were wronged. Just as Joseph responded in love to Mary, we need to respond in love to those who have hurt us.

Dear Father,
Sometimes, when I feel hurt, I want to retaliate. I want the other
person to experience pain, just as I have. But that isn't how You want
me to respond, is it? You want me to react in love, every single time.
That kind of love isn't easy.

Just as Joseph was hurt because of a misunderstanding, there are
times when I don't have all the information about a situation. Help
me to be like Joseph, responding in love even when I feel hurt, even
when I don't understand. Thank You for helping me to love others the
way You love them, no matter what. Amen.

Dear Father,

Thank You for Your generosity. You created the heavens and the earth and gave me all that I need to live a fulfilling life. You gave Your Son so that I could have a right relationship with You. But Your generosity didn't stop there. You continue giving and giving, waiting to pour out Your wisdom and blessings on all who seek You.

Please help me to follow Your example. I want to be generous to the people around me, without finding fault. Help me to be generous at Christmastime and all year long. I want to be wise and loving and patient and kind, just like You. Amen.

Giving Generously

But if any of you lacks wisdom, let him ask of God, who gives to all generously and
without reproach, and it will be given to him.
JAMES 1:5 NASB

We all love to be generous at Christmastime. We purchase lavish gifts for
our loved ones. We donate food, money, and clothing to various charities.
We give of our time, visiting hospitals and nursing homes. We even buy
extra treats for our pets.

Unfortunately, on December 26 we often become busy un-decorating
our trees, taking down the lights, and boxing up all our holiday knick-
knacks. We don't mean to put our generosity on hold for another year.
We're just distracted by other things.

It's a good thing God is generous 365 days a year. He generously gives
His wisdom to any who ask. He doesn't play favorites, He never holds
back, and He's never, ever too busy for us. He doesn't remind us of past
failures, and He never says, "I told you so. If you'd listened to Me last time,
you wouldn't be in this fix." It is His nature to be generous, and He stands
ready to shower us with wisdom and guidance and everything else we
need. All we have to do is ask.

Finding Joy

"If you keep My commandments, you will abide in My love....
These things I have spoken to you so that My joy may be in you,
and that your joy may be made full."
JOHN 15:10–11 NASB

During the holidays, we see the word *joy* everywhere. It is plastered on department store walls, hanging in lights over town squares, embossed in gold on the cover of greeting cards. Joy seems to be the mascot emotion of Christmastime.

And it should be. After all, Jesus came to teach us how to have joy. At Christmas we celebrate Jesus' arrival on earth; and He made it possible for us to know true joy. So why is it that, in spite of the word joy displayed everywhere, there is so much loneliness, emptiness, and depression? Why are people searching so desperately to find the joy that seems to bombard us from every side?

Well, it's possibly because we forget what Jesus taught us. We find joy by keeping the Father's commandments. We find joy by loving God with all our hearts, and loving other people as we love ourselves. Instead, we search for joy through selfish means, clamoring for attention and material possessions and recognition.

Just as the word *joy* stares us in the face during the holiday season, true joy in our lives is closer than we think. We find joy by doing what Jesus taught us to do: love.

Dear Father,

*Thank You for showing us how to have real joy in our lives. I don't
know why I waste my time seeking happiness through material things,
or through other people's admiration. I know that Jesus came to show
me the way to live a full, abundant, joy-filled life.*

*Funny how mixed up I can get things. I try to find joy by adding
things to my life, but real joy comes only when I give my life away.
Help me to follow Your example, loving You and loving others. As
I empty myself of me, I'll look for You to fill me up with Your joy.
Amen.*

Dear Father,
Thank You for the older, wiser, more experienced people You've placed in my life. Help me to give them the respect they deserve. I want to learn from their wisdom, knowing their understanding can help me avoid potential pitfalls in life. I want to benefit from their experiences.

As I grow older, help me to become wiser, too. Like Anna, I want to live every day of my life for You. Help me to speak of my experiences with others, so they can know You better. I want to be wise, and I want to share that wisdom with others. Amen.

Old Woman

There was also a prophetess, Anna.... She was very old; she had lived with her husband seven years after her marriage, and then was a widow until she was eighty-four. She never left the temple but worshiped night and day, fasting and praying Coming up to them at that very moment, she gave thanks to God and spoke about the child to all who were looking forward to the redemption of Jerusalem.
LUKE 2:36–38

Our society values youth and beauty. Everywhere we look, we see perfect, svelte bodies and wrinkle-free faces plastered on billboards and the sides of buses. Young actors and actresses have their own talk shows and promote their books. It doesn't seem to matter if they have any wisdom or life experience. They're beautiful, so we listen to them.

While many young people do have important messages, we are foolish to value their words over the ideas of older, wiser, more experienced people. The older a person is, the more they've lived. And the more they've lived, the more they've learned. We would be wise to find the aged people in our lives and hang on their every word. They have much to offer.

Anna was an old, childless widow, and God chose to use her as His mouthpiece. Even today, God often speaks through older people. We should listen closely; God may be trying to speak directly to us through their words.

Another Route

He sent them to Bethlehem and said, "Go and make a careful search for the child.
As soon as you find him, report to me, so that I too may go and worship him."...
And having been warned in a dream not to go back to Herod,
they returned to their country by another route.
MATTHEW 2:8, 12

Sometimes it's hard to know who we can trust and who we can't. After all, we vote for politicians because they seem honest, hardworking, and sincere. Later we often find that their sincerity has given way to lies and corruption. Before long, we start feeling like we can't believe a word anybody says.

But if we look to God, He will give us discernment. Though the men had every reason to obey Herod, God showed them Herod's true intent. These were wise men. They were certainly good, law-abiding citizens. Normally, they would have obeyed the king's orders. But in this case, God showed them a better way.

God wants us to obey our leaders, unless they tell us to do something contrary to God's Word. Even then, God wants us to seek peaceful alternatives to disobedience. The wise men didn't storm Herod's palace with accusations and insults. They simply went home another way. Whether we're figuring out whether to trust someone or wondering how to handle a difficult personality, we can look to God for answers. His ways are always the best ways.

Dear Father,
Thank You for giving me discernment. Sometimes it's hard to know
who I can trust, who I should believe, and who I should be wary of.
Help me to see people the way You do. Help me to recognize when
people are sincere and when they have false motives.

Even when I feel someone is insincere, help me not to treat them
with rudeness or harsh judgment. You are the one true judge—that's
not my place. Teach me to avoid evil, dishonest people, while treating
them with Your love when I have to be around them. Thank You for
helping me to act in wisdom. Amen.

Dear Father,
Thank You for Your goodness. You are so loving, so generous, so wise. . .
and yet I often keep Your goodness to myself. I don't know why I
hesitate to share Your love, for the news of that love is life-changing.

    Forgive me for keeping my mouth shut about You. I want to be
like those shepherds, taking every opportunity to share Your good news
and Your love with those around me. Help me to know when to speak
and with whom I should share. Give me wisdom to know what to say
and how to say it, so others will receive this message with joy. Amen.

Spread the Word

*When they had seen him, they spread the word concerning
what had been told them about this child.*
LUKE 2:17

The shepherds couldn't believe their eyes. They had searched and searched,
and they'd found God's Son lying in a manger, just as the angel said they
would. This was the One they had heard stories about. This was the One
they'd looked for their whole lives. This was the One for whom their
parents and grandparents and great-grandparents had waited.

After spending a few minutes looking at the baby, they knew they
couldn't keep this news to themselves. "Let's go tell everyone," they
whispered. After all, this news was life changing. God had kept His
promise and now dwelt among men. He was no longer distant and
unreachable. He was right there, and anyone who wanted to could see
Him, talk to Him, and have a relationship with Him.

Like those shepherds, we need to spread the word concerning God's
goodness. He dwells among us, through His Holy Spirit. He is accessible
to any who seek Him, and He loves us more than anything. This news is
too wonderful to keep to ourselves. We need to spread the word, letting
everyone know that God is here and wants to be intimately involved in
our lives.

Gentle and Kind

Be completely humble and gentle; be patient, bearing with one another in love.
EPHESIANS 4:2

One of the most humble, gentle pictures in scripture is that of Christ's birth. The King of heaven and earth, the One at whose command the winds change course, left His throne. He didn't choose to make His appearance at a palace but in a stable. Now that's humility.

Rather than showing up with a scepter and a sword, the Son of God became a helpless, tiny baby. Instead of judging us, He put Himself at our mercy. Now He wants us to follow His example.

Sure, we all feel we deserve things that we don't get, but that doesn't mean we have to demand them. Just as Christ left His throne for a smelly stable, we can lay aside our rightful claims and cheerfully accept a lower position. Instead of judging others and focusing on their faults, we can love them in spite of their faults. After all, isn't that what Christ did for us?

This holiday season and every day throughout the year, let's follow Christ's example. Let's lay aside our claims to greatness, lay aside our desires for importance, and choose to focus instead on the needs and desires of those around us. Let us stop concentrating on the faults of others and instead show them kindness, gentleness, and love.

Dear Father,

When I compare Your actions to my own, I am ashamed. You have every right to be proud, yet You are the picture of humility. You are the Divine Judge, and You alone have the authority to pick apart my faults and make me feel like a total failure, but You don't. Instead, You are gentle with me, showering me with kindness, mercy, and forgiveness.

I want to be like You. Help me to be humble in my relationships. Instead of trying to be the important one, help me to make other people—even the ones I don't like—feel important. Instead of finding fault, help me to be gentle, merciful, and kind. Amen.

Dear Father,

Thank You for loving me. I can't understand why You would pay such a price for me; it doesn't make any sense. Then again, it makes perfect sense when I think of who You are. You are love. Everything You are, everything You do, is a direct result of that love for Your children.

Help me to love others. Real love, true love is hard. In order to love, I sometimes have to sacrifice my pride, or my goals, or my comfort in favor of another. I don't understand that kind of love, but I know the rewards of such love are great. I know that it is only through that kind of love that I can be made into the person You created me to be. Lord, I want to love that way. I want to love like You love. Amen.

This Is Love

This is love: not that we loved God, but that he loved us and sent his Son as an atoning sacrifice for our sins. Dear friends, since God so loved us, we also ought to love one another.
1 JOHN 4:10–11

The best Christmas gifts are the ones that say, "I love you," to the recipient. Oh, any gift is nice. It's fun to tear the paper off the package, even if it's just a soap-on-a-rope or another pair of fuzzy slippers. It's the thought that counts. But when the giver knows I've wanted a soap-on-a-rope since the fourth grade, but never got one, or that my feet are always cold and my old slippers got chewed up by the dog, those gifts send a true message of love.

True love gives with the recipient in mind. God demonstrated love when He sent His Son to do something that needed doing—something that we could not do for ourselves. He paid much too high a price for me, showing His love sacrificially, to have me treat such a gift with flippancy and disregard. The one thing He asked as a "thank You" is for me to love as He has loved. He wants me to love other people. Sacrificially. With them in mind.

That kind of love takes humility. It takes patience and kindness and gentleness and forgiveness, time and again. Yet it's a small thing, really, considering what He did for me.

Prayers
of Gratitude

Thank You

Give thanks to the LORD, for he is good;
his love endures forever.
1 CHRONICLES 16:34

All too often, our prayers become like a child's never-ending letter to Santa. "Dear Lord, I'd like a new job and a new house. I'd like for my husband to be nicer to me. I'd like to lose ten pounds. Oh, and umm. . .I'd really like for my headaches to go away."

There's nothing wrong with telling God what we want. He longs for us to come to Him, to talk to Him about everything that is going on in our lives. But often we forget to say those two little words that are so important: Thank You.

God loves us beyond comprehension. His love is never-ending. Nothing can change it or stop it. No matter what, God will continue to shower us with good things. But when we fail to give thanks, we become like a self-centered child, asking for more and more and more, and never showing gratitude for the gifts we've already received.

Today and every day, let's make it a point to notice the things God has already done for us. Before we ask Him for another thing, let's take a moment to say, "Thank You."

Dear Father,

Thank You for Your never-ending love for me. You have blessed me in ways I can't measure. If I tried to make a list of all the wonderful things You have done for me, I'd run out of paper before I'd run out of list.

Please know that I am grateful for every good thing You send my way. I'm sorry that I sometimes forget to say, "Thank You." Remind me to notice all the wonderful things You do for me. Help me express my gratitude by living each moment for You, sharing Your goodness with everyone I meet.

I love You, and thanks for everything. Amen.

Dear Father,

Thank You for sending Your Son to us. He came, not to be an earthly king, but to be the King of my heart. Help me to make room for Him, allowing Him to rule my thoughts, my words, my actions, and every part of my life.

Lord, Jesus didn't come in the expected package. The Israelites expected a rich ruler, and He showed up as a poor working-class man. Likewise, many of my greatest blessings don't come in a pretty package. Help me to recognize the hidden gifts You send my way. Help me to be grateful for them. Amen.

Great Expectations

"He will be great and will be called the Son of the Most High. The Lord God will give him the throne of his father David, and he will reign over the house of Jacob forever; his kingdom will never end."
LUKE 1:32–33

Israel had long awaited its promised king. They knew He was coming. God had told them so. They expected a mighty king who would rule over all the earth and lead Israel to greatness. But when He finally arrived, they missed Him. He didn't come to be an earthly king, but a heavenly one. He came not to rule a nation, but to rule men's hearts. Many people missed out on the blessings of getting to rub shoulders with God's Son, of getting to be close friends with Him, simply because He didn't live up to their expectations.

Sometimes we make the same mistake. We have certain expectations for our lives—expectations of wealth, success, and happiness. But often God's greatest blessings don't come wrapped in glamorous packages. The most difficult of circumstances can prove to be a great treasure, if it was ordained by God. We need to be careful not to overlook the gifts God has placed in our lives, simply because they don't fit our desires or expectations.

What's in a Name?

For to us a child is born, to us a son is given, and the government will be on his shoulders. And he will be called Wonderful Counselor, Mighty God, Everlasting Father, Prince of Peace.

ISAIAH 9:6

Expectant parents often spend many hours choosing a name for their coming child. After all, names are important. A person's name follows him throughout life and can provide a powerful first impression to others. A name often reflects that person's character or personality.

Just as parents want their child's name to make a positive impression on others, God wanted His Son's name to reflect His character and His personality. He chose many names for Jesus, and each name reminds us of a different aspect of His nature. Each name reminds us how much He loves us.

Jesus is Wonderful. He is our Counselor and helps us make wise choices. He is the Mighty God—able to move mountains and change hearts. He is a Father to the fatherless, and He offers peace to those who are in distress. Jesus has many more names, as well. He is our Provider, our Healer, our Friend. Each name provides insight into who He is, and allows us to know Him more.

Dear Father,

Thank You for giving Jesus so many names. Each name is a reminder to me of how much You love me. As I remember Jesus' names, help me to remember that You want to offer that character trait to me. You want to be my Counselor, guiding me when I feel lost or confused. You want to be my Provider, so I won't have to worry about getting the things I need. You want to be my Friend, so I won't feel lonely. You want to offer me peace when my life is in chaos. Thank You for giving me so many gifts, all wrapped up in Your Son. Amen.

Dear Father,

I am amazed that You—the God of the universe—notice me. When I think of it, I feel overwhelmed. After all, when I look in the mirror, I see a flawed, weak, sinful person. I don't see anything noteworthy.

Yet You are mindful of me. You watch me as I sleep; You drive with me in the car; You travel with me on my errands. You even walk with me through the grocery store. You love me so much that You want to be an intimate part of my life.

Thank You, Father. Like Mary, my soul glorifies You, and my spirit rejoices that You have taken an interest in me. I love You. Amen.

Getting Noticed

*"My soul glorifies the Lord and my spirit rejoices in God my Savior,
for he has been mindful of the humble state of his servant."*
LUKE 1:46–48

Have you ever felt like God has forgotten about you? Sometimes when
life seems to be caving in on us, we find ourselves waving our arms and
frantically trying to get His attention. "Hey, God! I could use a little help
here, please!"

But all the kicking and screaming and frantically trying to get Him
to notice us is pointless. Oh, not pointless because He ignores us. Pointless
because we already have His full attention.

You see, He created you and me, and He loves us more than He loves
His own life. No matter how humble or lowly or pitiful our state may be,
He takes notice of us. He is interested in every detail of our lives, and He
wants to bless us more than we can imagine.

Just look at Mary. There was nothing about her that made her
special—at least not in the world's eyes. She was young, probably poor,
probably uneducated. Yet God noticed her and chose her to be the mother
of His Son. He had a great purpose and plan for her life.

He has a great purpose and plan for your life and my life, as well. He
loves us. He notices us. And He is waiting to pour out His blessings.

Good Gifts

Every good thing given and every perfect gift is from above,
coming down from the Father of lights.
JAMES 1:17 NASB

Each holiday season, we spend hours traipsing through the malls and the department stores in search of the perfect gift for everyone on our lists. Sometimes we just can't find the right thing for Uncle Bob or Cousin Thelma. Other times, we find so many "perfect" gifts, we can't make up our minds which one to purchase.

Aren't you glad God knows the perfect gifts for each of His children? He gives them every day of the year, too! Whether it is a glorious sunset, a perfect cup of coffee, or a smile from a friend, God sends exactly what we need at exactly the right moment. Sometimes He sends these gifts because we really need them. But more often He showers us with His blessings simply because He loves us, and He likes to see us smile.

The best gift He gave to us was His Son, Jesus Christ. He sent His only child to live for us, so we would know how to live. Then He allowed that child to die, so that we wouldn't have to. Yes, Christ was, is, and always will be the perfect gift. Everything else is just embellishment.

Dear Father,
Thank You for overwhelming me with Your perfect gifts. Regardless
of whether or not I deserve them, You keep sending me reflections
of Your grace each and every day. The sun shines, the birds sing, the
soft snow falls like a blanket on the world. . .those are all reminders
of Your love for me.

Father, Thank You for Your most precious gift—Your Son. I know
You sent Him to pay the price for my sins, for You knew the price was
too high for me. I could never have afforded it. I don't know if I'll
ever completely understand that kind of love, but I'm so grateful for
it, all the same. Amen.

Dear Father,

I am amazed that You want to be with me. I'm overwhelmed that You went to such great lengths, sending Your only Son to be born and live and die, to be rejected and spat upon and humiliated, so that I could have an intimate relationship with You. I don't know how to express my thanks, Lord.

Thank You for being there every time I call. Thank You for staying so close that You can hear my softest whisper—even the whispers of my heart. I want to honor You with my life, so that You will always feel welcomed in my presence.

I love You, Lord. Amen.

God with Us

God With Us

All this took place to fulfill what the Lord had said through the prophet:
"The virgin will be with child and will give birth to a son,
and they will call him Immanuel—which means, God with us."
MATTHEW 1:22–23

Before Jesus came, God was pretty inaccessible. Oh, He was there. But to get to Him, to be in right standing with Him, people had to jump through a lot of hoops. They had to make sacrifices and follow all the rules to the letter. And they couldn't actually go into His presence all by themselves. Nope. The Holy of Holies—God's presence—was reserved for the high priests, and no one else.

Jesus changed all of that. Jesus—fully man and fully God—came to be with us. When He was born, people could finally see and touch and speak with and laugh with and hug God. No longer was He separated from all of us. Jesus was God in the flesh, and He was right in the midst of us.

Because of what Christ did for us on the cross, God is still with us. We don't have to jump through hoops or make sacrifices or rely on the high priest to talk to God for us. He is right there with us. He hears every word; He feels the beat of our hearts. All we need to do is acknowledge His presence, because He is already there.

Extravagant Gift

*This is how God showed his love among us: He sent his one and only Son
into the world that we might live through him.*
1 JOHN 4:9

When our children are young, we teach them to show gratitude for
the gifts that are given to them. "Say 'thank you,'" we whisper. At our
prompting, they smile sheepishly and express their thanks. It doesn't
matter how much the gift cost; we want our children to be grateful.

Yet cost matters, for cost represents sacrifice. If we purchase something
on the clearance table at the dollar store, that gift doesn't usually represent the
same sacrifice as if we scrimp and save for months to purchase just the right
gift. If someone shows little gratitude for a gift that costs next-to-nothing,
well, it's not that big of a deal. But if we really sacrifice so that someone can
have a special gift, it goes without saying—we'd like that person to show a
little gratitude.

God gave us the greatest gift. His gift cost Him more than any gift
we've ever purchased for anyone. It cost His Son's life. He gave such a gift
because of His great love for us. With that in mind, I want the rest of my
life to be lived in gratitude to Him.

Dear Father,

Thank You for giving such an extravagant gift to me. No matter what I do, I know I'll never be able to thank You adequately for such a sacrifice. You gave Your Son's life so that I might live. Truly I can't even comprehend such love.

Though I don't understand the depth of Your love for me, I am grateful for it all the same. I know I can never repay the debt I owe. You don't want me to repay it, for it was a gift. But Lord, I do want You to know how thankful I am to You. In exchange for Your Son's life, I want to give back my own life—living every moment for You. Amen.

Dear Father,

Thank You for keeping Your promises to me. Like the wise men, I want to follow You on this journey called life. I want to stay the course, never veering to the right or the left. I know that You have wonderful plans for my life. As long as I stay close to You, You'll lead me to the fulfillment of those plans.

The wise men were rewarded when they saw Your Son with their own eyes. I'll get to see Him, too, as long as I follow You. Thank You for leading me, for smoothing out the path for me, and for making it possible for me to live out my highest calling—to become the person You created me to be. Amen.

Overjoyed

The star they had seen in the east went ahead of them until it stopped over the place where the child was. When they saw the star, they were overjoyed.
MATTHEW 2:9–10

We can all relate to the joy felt when a goal is finally met or a long-awaited gift is finally received. That moment when our diploma is placed in our hands, representing years of hard work, or the feeling when our newborn child is placed in our arms for the first time fills us with awe. When the anticipation of an event finally collides with reality, we are both thrilled and overwhelmed.

That's how the wise men felt when they realized their dreams had finally come true. They were overjoyed. They were probably filled with gratitude to the One who had led them safely to the realization of their hopes and dreams. They had stayed the course; God had delivered His promise; and they were thrilled and thankful.

Friends, God always delivers on His promises. Like those wise men, if we stay the course by drawing near to God, our dreams of becoming all He created us to be will collide with His perfect will for us. God wants to help us arrive at that moment when He says, "Well done."

Promises Kept

Simeon took him in his arms and praised God, saying: "Sovereign Lord,
as you have promised, you now dismiss your servant in peace."
LUKE 2:28–29

Simeon was an old man. He loved God very much, and the Holy Spirit
had revealed to him that he wouldn't die before he saw God's Son. He
knew the best place for that to happen was at the temple, so he spent a
lot of time there, waiting for God to fulfill His promise—both to him
personally and to Israel.

When Mary and Joseph showed up with baby Jesus in their arms,
Simeon knew God had kept His promise. There was never any doubt
in Simeon's mind; it was only a matter of when the promise would be
fulfilled. Now the old man could die in peace. He had seen the newborn
Messiah.

Like Simeon, we can live in excited expectation of the good things
God will do for us. God has made us many generous promises, and
He will keep every single one of them. He has promised peace and joy
and wisdom to all who seek Him. He has promised to supply all our
needs. Like Simeon, we can spend each day of our lives looking for those
promises to be fulfilled. And like Simeon, we won't be disappointed.

Dear Father,

Thank You for the many promises You have made to me. Sometimes I forget that You always keep Your promises. I worry and fret, wondering how I'll meet this need or that one, wondering if I'll ever find peace. I try to fulfill those promises on my own, instead of waiting patiently, with gratitude, to see how You will fulfill them.

Lord, I want to be like Simeon. I want to live each day knowing that You will keep all of Your promises. I want to live in eager expectation of those promises, knowing that You love to bless me, that You love to see me smile. Thank You for meeting all my needs and many of my wants. Thank You for the things You'll do for me today. Like Simeon, I'm watching and waiting. Amen.

Dear Father,

I am amazed that You would sacrifice so much for me. I don't understand it, and I certainly don't deserve it. Yet I'm so glad You loved me enough to give up Your place in glory, just to be with me.

Lord, sometimes I forget that You truly are with me. I forget that You came so that I would never have to live a moment without You. Help me to draw on Your power, Your peace, and Your love, which You placed within me when I became Your child.

Thank You, Father. I love You. Amen.

Three Little Words

"The virgin will be with child and will give birth to a son, and they will call him Immanuel"—which means, "God with us."
MATTHEW 1:23

Three little words, one syllable each, with less than ten letters in the whole description. . .how can three tiny little words hold such power? Yet all the power of the universe is contained in that one short statement: "God with us."

God, who created the heavens and the earth and every living thing. . . with us. God, who commands the storms and the sun and the moon. . . with us. God, the King of kings and Lord of lords, the Wonderful Counselor, the Everlasting Father, chose to leave His heavenly throne and all His splendor and come down to rub elbows with the likes of you and me.

Why would He do that? It doesn't make any sense.

There is only one reason He would do that: love. That kind of love holds both power and peace. When we become children of God, we hold that very power within us. We hold that peace within our grasp. Because He loved us, He became like us. And because He loved us, we can become like Him.

ALL YEAR LONG

Dear Father,
Thank You for the Christmas season, which brings
reminders of Your great love for us. As the season
draws to an end and I begin to pack away the lights
and ornaments, I don't want to pack away the
message of Your love. Help me to be a messenger of
Your grace, mercy, and kindness all year long,
to everyone I meet.
Like Mary, I am grateful that You, the King of
kings, have noticed me. Like the shepherds, I want
to tell everyone about You. Like the angels, I want to
sing of Your goodness to all the world. Help me to
carry Your peace and Your love with me,
every day of the year. Amen.